ITALIAN POLITICS
ADJUSTMENT UNDER
DURESS

MARTIN J. BULL
AND
JAMES L. NEWELL

polity

First published in 2005 by Polity Press

Polity Press
65 Bridge Street
Cambridge CB2 1UR, UK

Polity Press
350 Main Street
Malden, MA 02148, USA

ISBN: 0-7456-1298-9
ISBN: 0-7456-1299-7 (pb)

A catalogue record for this book is available from the British Library.

Typeset in 10 on 12 pt Sabon
by SNP Best-set Typesetter Ltd, Hong Kong
Printed and bound in Great Britain by MPG Books Ltd, Bodmin, Cornwall

For further information on Polity, visit our website: www.polity.co.uk

CONTENTS

ACKNOWLEDGEMENTS

We would like to thank various bodies whose generous support made the researching and writing of this book possible: the Leverhulme Trust; the University of Salford Research Investment Fund; the Christopher Hale Memorial Fund; the European Studies Research Institute of the University of Salford; the Department of Political and Social Sciences and the library of the European University Institute, Florence; the *Biblioteca Nazionale* (National Library) in Florence; the Italian Chamber of Deputies Library Service; the Election Services Unit of the Italian Ministry of the Interior; and the *Corte dei Conti* (Italian Financial Audit Office).

For their kind permission to reproduce tables or extracts of their publications, we thank: La Découverte for tables 2.1, 2.3 and 11.1, which are reproduced from Giovanni Balcet, *L'économie italienne* © Editions La Découverte, Paris 1995; and the OECD for tables 2.5, 2.6, 2.9, 10.4, 10.5, 11.2, 11.3, which are adapted from tables found in: *OECD Economic Surveys: Italy – Volume 2003, Issue 13*, © OECD, 2003; *OECD Territorial Reviews Italy*, © OECD, 2001; and *Review dell'OCSE della riforma della regolazione in Italia*, © OECD, 2001.

Our thanks go to Polity for supporting this project throughout, and to the two anonymous readers for their very useful suggestions on how to improve the text. We also wish to acknowledge our debt to the broader community of Italianist scholars who influenced our ideas and research whilst we were writing this book. While, as our book makes clear, there is a lively debate over exactly how much has changed in Italian politics since the early 1990s, there is little doubt that the study of Italian politics has been revolutionized in that period. A cursory comparison of the body of work produced before the 1990s (see Tranfaglia (1994); Bull (1996a); and Donovan (1998) with the explosion in the number of publications since, bears testimony to the impact of the Italian political scene on its academic study. Italianists have been provided with fresh opportunities to generate new agendas for research, and this has brought them together on a much more frequent basis than before. In the course of this research, we have participated in countless conferences, panels, workshops and seminars in Britain, Italy, other European countries and North America, dedicated to understanding the trajectory of the change that Italian politics has been undergoing. In particular, we would draw attention to the extraordinary hospitality Italian political scientists give to foreign scholars researching Italian politics. The formers' encouragement of and enthusiasm for our intellectual efforts should not overshadow the importance of their own work, which we wish to acknowledge here. Our book would be all the poorer if it had not been influenced by their high quality research and illuminating discussions.

Finally, we thank Maria, Francesca, Anthony, Serena, Vicky, Robin and Tom. Their indirect contribution to the writing of this book is inestimable.

Martin Bull and James Newell
November 2004

TABLES

FIGURES

ABBREVIATIONS

ACLI	Associazione Cattolica dei Lavoratori Italiani (Italian Workers' Catholic Association)
AD	Alleanza Democratica (Democratic Alliance)
AGIP	Azienda Generale Italiana Petroli (Italian General Petrol Company)
AN	Alleanza Nazionale (National Alliance)
ANIC	Azienda Nazionale Idrogenazione Combustibili (National Corporation for Combustible Hydrogenation)
BNL	Banca Nazionale del Lavoro (National Bank of Work)
BR	Brigate Rosse (Red Brigades)
CAF	'Craxi-Andreotti-Forlani'
CAP	Common Agricultural Policy
CARIPLO	Cassa di Risparmio delle Province Lombarde (Savings Bank of the Provinces of Lombardy)
CCD	Centro Cristiano Democratico (Christian Democratic Centre)
CCD–CDU	Centro Cristiano Democratico–Cristiani Democratici Uniti (Christian Democratic Centre–Christian Democratic Union)
CDL	Casa delle Libertà (House of Freedoms)
CDU	Cristiani Democratici Uniti (Christian Democratic Union)
CEI	Conferenza Episcopale Italiana (Italian Episcopal Conference)
CESIS	Comitato Esecutivo per i Servizi di Informazione e di Sicurezza (Secret Services Executive Committee)
CGIL	Confederazione Generale Italiana del Lavoro (General Confederation of Italian Labour)
CIA	Central Intelligence Agency
CIPE	Comitato Interministeriale per la Pianificazione Economica (Interministerial Committee for Economic Planning)
CIPI	Comitato Interministeriale per la Politica Industriale (Interministerial Committee for Industrial Policy)
CISL	Confederazione Italiana Sindacati Lavoratori (Italian Confederation of Workers' Unions)

CIT	Compagnia Italiana Turismo (Italian Tourism Company)
CONSOB	Commissione Nazionale per le Società e la Borsa (National Commission for Enterprises and the Stock Exchange)
C-S	Cristiano Sociali (Social Christians)
CSM	Consiglio Superiore della Magistratura (High Council of the Judiciary)
DC	Democrazia Cristiana (Christian Democratic Party)
DEM EUR	Democrazia Europea (European Democracy)
DL	Democrazia e Libertà (Democracy and Liberty)
DP	Democrazia Proletaria (Proletarian Democracy)
DS	Democratici di Sinistra (Left Democrats)
EC	European Community
EEC	European Economic Community
EFIM	Ente Partecipazioni e Finanziamento Industria Manifatturiera (Agency for the Financing of State Manufacturing Industry)
EGAM	Ente Autonomo di Gestione per le Aziende Minerarie Metallurgiche (Agency for the Management of Metallurgic and Mining Firms)
EMS	European Monetary System
EMU	Economic and Monetary Union
ENEL	Ente Nazionale per l'Energia Elettrica in Italia (National Electricity Corporation)
ENI	Ente Nazionale Idrocarburi (National Hydrocarbon Corporation)
ERM	Exchange Rate Mechanism
EU	European Union
FDI	foreign direct investment
FI	Forza Italia
FIM	Federazione Italiana Metalmeccanici (Italian Metalworkers' Federation)
FIOM	Federazione Impiegati Operai Metallurgici (Federation of Workers in the Metallurgic Industry)
GATT	General Agreement on Tariffs and Trade
GEPI	Società di Gestione e Partecipazioni Industriali (Organization for the Management of State-Controlled Industry)
ICI	Imposta comunale sugli immobili (Local property tax)
IFI	Istituto Finanziario Italiano (Italian Financial Institute)
IGC	Intergovernmental Conference
IMF	International Monetary Fund
IMI	Istituto Mobiliare Italiano (Italian Credit Institute)
INA	Istituto Nazionale delle Assicurazioni (National Insurance Institute)
INSUD	Società Finanziaria Nuove Iniziative per il Sud (Financial Company for New Initiatives in the South)
IRB	independent regulatory body
IRI	Istituto per la Ricostruzione Industriale (Institute for Industrial Reconstruction)
ISTAT	Istituto Nazionale di Statistica (National Statistical Institute)

ITANES	Italian National Election Study
IV	Italia dei Valori (Italy of Values)
LN	Lega Nord, or Lega (Northern League)
LP	Lista Pannella (Pannella List)
MSI	Movimento Sociale Italiano (Italian Social Movement)
MSFT	Movimento Sociale-Fiamma Tricolore (Tri-Coloured Flame)
NATO	North Atlantic Treaty Organization
NVP	'non-vote party'
OECD	Organization for Economic Co-operation and Development
OEEC	Organization for European Economic Co-operation
P2	Propaganda Due ('Propaganda Two' Masonic lodge)
PCI	Partito Comunista Italiano (Italian Communist Party)
PCM	Presidenza del Consiglio dei Ministri (Prime Minister's Office)
Pd'A	Partito d'Azione (Party of Action)
Pd CI	Partito dei Comunisti Italiani (Party of Italian Communists)
PDL	Partito Democratico del Lavoro (Democratic Party of Labour)
PDS	Partito Democratico della Sinistra (Democratic Party of the Left)
PDS–SE	PDS–Sinistrà Europea (PDS–European Left)
PdUP	Partito Democratico dell'Unità Proletaria (Democratic Party of Proletarian Unity)
PLD	Polo Liberal-Democratico (Liberal Democratic Alliance)
PLI	Partito Liberale Italiano (Italian Liberal Party)
PNM	Partito Nazionale Monarchico (National Monarchical Party)
PPI	Partito Popolare Italiano (Italian People's Party)
PR	Partito Radicale (Radical Party)
PRI	Partito Repubblicano Italiano (Italian Republican Party)
P. Sardo d'Az.	Partito Sardo d'Azione (Sardinian Action Party)
PSDI	Partito Socialista Democratico Italiano (Italian Social Democratic Party)
PSI	Partito Socialista Italiano (Italian Socialist Party)
PSIUP	Partito Socialista di Unità Proletaria (Italian Socialist Party of Workers' Unity)
PSLI	Partito Socialista Lavoratori Italiani (Italian Socialist Workers' Party)
PSU	Partito Socialista Unito (United Socialist Party)
RAI	Radiotelevisione Italiana (Italian Radio and Television)
RC	Rifondazione Comunista (Communist Refoundation)
Rete	Rete (Network)
RI	Rinnovamento Italiano (Italian Renewal)
RS	Rinascita Socialista (Socialist Renewal)
SDI	Socialisti Democratici Italiani (Italian Democratic Socialists)
SEA	Single European Act
SI	Socialisti Italiani (Italian Socialists)
SIP	Società Italiana per l'Esercizio delle Telecommunicazioni (Italian National Telecommunications Company)
SMEs	Small and medium-sized enterprises
SNAM	Società Nazionale Metanodotti (National Gas Pipeline Corporation)

STET	Società Finanziaria Telefonica per Azioni (Holding Company for the Telecommunications Sector)
SVP	Südtirolervolkspartei (South Tyrolese People's Party)
TAR	Tribunale Amministrativo Regionale (Regional Administrative Tribunal)
UD	Unione Democratica (Democratic Union)
UdC	Unione di Centro (Union of the Centre)
UDC	Unione dei Democratici Cristiani (Union of Christian Democrats)
UDEUR	Unione dei Democratici per l'Europa (Union of Democrats for Europe)
UDR	Unione Democratica per la Repubblica (Democratic Union for the Republic)
UIL	Unione Italiana dei Lavoratori (Italian Workers' Union)
UILM	Unione Italiani Lavoratori Metalmeccanici (Union of Italian Metalworkers)
Ulivo	Ulivo (Olive-tree Alliance)
UMI	Unione dei Magistrati Italiani (Union of Italian Magistrates)

INTRODUCTION

Writing about the contemporary politics of a nation-state presents two problems. The first concerns the spread of subject matter, or which subject areas to incorporate. It goes without saying that understanding the politics of a nation requires an analysis that goes beyond the study of its formal institutions; yet, there is a choice in what else to include. The immediate issue is less one of relevance (for all subject areas will have their claim) than of space, and, in this context, how much weight an author wants to give to providing an *interpretation* or *explanation* as well as a description of the political system. Put another way, while it might be feasible to include a *comprehensive* range of subjects, this would inevitably be at the cost of interpretation and explanation, since the space that could be devoted to each would be severely curtailed. The danger would arise of a patchwork treated in a largely descriptive manner. Alternatively, reducing the subject areas too far with the aim of presenting a clear interpretation of the material runs the risk of excluding key areas on which the interpretation hangs (or on which it might be unhinged). Obviously, readers will have to judge for themselves whether this book manages to meet these competing demands successfully. Suffice it to say that we have attempted to convey an interpretation of Italian politics since 1945 which goes beyond the specifically (or formally) political, but does not spread itself so widely as to lose its explanatory power.

The second problem relates to the temporal period being analysed and what, broadly speaking, has happened in that period. Since a political science text is not a history book, it is confronted with the issue of what time frame to use for the analysis. On the one hand, such a text would be expected to convey a description and interpretation of *today's* politics; yet, if it is limited only to this, it is providing no more than a snap shot of the present which could fade very quickly. Moreover, while *describing* the politics of today without historical context is possible, providing an *interpretation* or *explanation* without it is certainly not. For this reason, most books attempt to locate current events within a broader time frame. In doing so, they are in a position to identify the essential and enduring characteristics of a polity. However, the ease or difficulty with which this problem can be addressed will depend on the degree of change that a polity has undergone in that time frame, something which is vividly apparent in the Italian case.

It is now conventional wisdom that the dramatic events of the early 1990s in Italian politics prompted a crisis, ending the 'old regime' and ushering in a period of transition that is still ongoing. This is popularly (as well as academically) expressed in the notions of First and Second Republic: 'the "Second Republic" may yet be unborn; the "First Republic" is, equally obviously, dead' (Newell 2000b: 185). The general consensus is that, while the essential characteristics of the First Republic have largely disappeared, the emergence of a Second Republic is dependent on institutional reform through constitutional revision. Consequently, as long as this has not been achieved, Italian politics remain in a state of transition. This makes the issue of the time frame problematic, if it is the case that 'any political transition, in the wider institutional and constitutional sense, is the interval between one regime and another' (Pasquino 2000b: 202). As Pasquino elsewhere (2001b: 324–5) notes, 'Writing a book on the Italian political system has never been easy. To attempt to do so right in the middle of a transition is a hazardous operation that is merit-worthy only in the event of the book succeeding' (this in a critique of a book that he felt had not succeeded). In this situation, one envies the Italian politics texts published on the cusp of (or just after) the dramatic changes began, where the time frame was apparently unproblematic, and the books could stand as historical records of the so-called First Republic.[1] Certainly, if the key theme of politics texts written before the 1990s was to explain why so little had (or could) change, then the task of the new generation of texts must be to document and explain how much has changed.

One approach to the problem would be to root the analysis only in the last decade, but that would run the risk noted above of the absence of an explanatory context or longer view. How is it possible to capture and explain a 'moving target' such as a 'transition' without knowledge of what went before? The analysis would amount effectively to a snap shot of the past decade.[2] An alternative approach would be to organize the whole book around the idea of a transition: a first section on what went before, a second section on why it changed, and a third on what has changed so far.[3] This effective incorporation into the transition literature may seem to be an obvious course to follow, yet, from a comparative, non-Italian viewpoint, it is also potentially problematic. Not only would it depart from the traditional and accepted format of texts of this nature; it would also tend to make Italy an exceptional case, and it is precisely the assumption of 'Italian exceptionalism' which comparative political science has been attempting to overcome in the past generation. Our approach, therefore, is different to both of these, while at the same time not radically diverging from convention.

Echoing Allum and Newell (2003: 189), we proceed on the basis of a distinction between the formal constitutional order and the broader political system. It is now a commonplace that constitutions, while structuring power, do not necessarily reflect accurately its distribution. Institutional relationships develop over time and are influenced by various factors that go beyond the Constitution. In Italy, a distinction has long been drawn between the 'formal constitution' and the 'material constitution', the latter referring to the 'political values' and 'institutional aims' underlying a legal order, as well as the prevailing political order or organization of public powers.[4] In Italy, while the period since the early 1990s has not produced a formal constitutional revision – or significant institutional reform beyond that of the electoral system (in 1993–4) and the regional system (in 2000) – the political system more broadly understood has nevertheless experienced significant (and ongoing) changes. It follows, therefore, that, while recognizing the importance in Italy of the formal constitutional order and attempts to reform it, the focus of an analysis of political change should be, in keeping with political science tradition, on the political system more broadly understood.

This distinction, of course, does not necessarily preclude organizing the book around the notion of 'before' and 'after' (the dramatic changes of the early 1990s). Accepting or rejecting this depends on one's overall assessment of the significance of the changes that have occurred. Evidently, if one is analysing a single sector of a polity, then a chronological organization makes sense, because an assessment of the extent of change and continuity is more straightforward.[5] However, assessing the political system overall is more complex, especially the wider the 'spread' adopted.[6] Moreover, even if one can make a clear case for a 'revolution' – in some 'meaningful sense of the word' (Ginsborg 1996a: 35) – having occurred in the political system as a whole, there are few revolutions that leave everything unchanged, and few that proceed at the same pace across all sectors of the polity at once. The most visible aspects of the 'old regime' may topple quickly (politicians, parties), but other sectors may be subject to very different levels and speeds of change. The important point is to be able to identify and distinguish between these diverse levels of change (and continuity) in different sectors of the polity. This is better done by a thematic approach to the post-war period as a whole, but one that none the less embeds within each theme the 1990s as a watershed, even where this watershed might be more apparent than real, or where change is occurring much more slowly than in other sectors.

Each chapter, therefore, is linked by a common theme. The chapter proceeds on the assumption that the 1990s mark a turning point; it analyses the post-war characteristics until the early 1990s, and then documents the changes that have occurred since the 1990s and are ongoing, as well as identifying the resistances to change and the continuities with the past. This provides a more fragmented picture of the Italian polity than texts based on a 'before and after' method, but also, we think, a more accurate one. It is also, we believe, an approach that rises to Pasquino's challenge of writing an overarching account of Italian politics during a period of considerable political change. Our approach does not reject the idea that the basic characteristics that shaped Italian politics in the post-war period have changed fundamentally during the 1990s, and that therefore it is accurate to speak of the end of the 'First Republic'. At the same time, this transformation of the *generality* is composed of differential degrees of change at the *specific* sectoral levels, and our purpose is to disentangle and analyse these sectors. This approach, however, also calls for some kind of overview or synthesis – an 'entanglement' of these sectors – in order to provide the reader with an overall picture of change in the Italian polity, against which the more fragmented picture may be evaluated. This is done in chapter 1 (to which we now turn), through a 'historical context', which, as outlined in the chapter's first pages, differs from the sort of historical chapters usually provided in a book of this sort.

Understanding Political Change in Post-War Italy

Introduction

There is a precedent in books of this sort to begin with a historical context, focusing on the imprint that early phases of Italian history might have left on the Italian Republic.[1] The historical context adopted here, however, is somewhat different. While not denying the importance of the liberal and Fascist orders that preceded the Republic, we have resisted the temptation to provide historical descriptions of these earlier phases, with an aim to providing a context of a different nature. This reasoning is prompted by the dramatic nature of the changes in the early 1990s. If these changes mark a watershed in the Italian Republic and the beginning of some form of transition from a First to a Second Republic, then the traditional approach to the historical context needs, in our view, to be adjusted. For if students of politics needed (and still need) some idea of the historical legacy of the phases preceding the Italian First Republic, the same argument applies to the emerging Second Republic. Yet, at the same time, as argued in the Introduction, we believe it premature to write a book of this sort on the basis of the last ten years only, which would mean reducing the period before the 1990s to nothing more than a (further) historical context. In our view, the period prior to the 1990s must be integrated into each chapter in order to explain the 'what, why and how' of Italy's current political change.

This challenge can be successfully met by providing a historical context which, besides analysing the legacy of the pre-First Republic phases, is also extended across *the same chronological period covered by the thematic chapters*. In this way, we can provide a more coherent picture overall, not only of the anomalous nature of the Italian political system of the First Republic and why it came to an end, but also of the change that the Italian political system is currently undergoing (since the change can be viewed through the prism of the development of the First Republic). Moreover, since this book is based on the view that a comprehensive understanding of a liberal democracy is not possible outside of its economic context, this politico-historical context will be complemented with an analogous chapter on the post-war Italian economy (chapter 2).

This chapter is therefore divided into four sections. The first analyses the importance of the post-war settlement and its impact on the subsequent development of the Republic, and to what extent the 'break' with the past was compromised. The second section analyses the nature of the Italian political system as it developed until the end of the 1980s. The third section analyses the long-term contradictions embedded in the system and how short-term factors assisted in exploding these contradictions. The final section then reviews the nature of the political change that the system is undergoing today.

THE POST-WAR SETTLEMENT

The development of the Italian Republic was heavily conditioned by the nature of the post-war settlement of 1944–8. This period was characterized by a contradictory and changing mix of two political fault lines: anti-fascism and anti-communism. If the first pushed towards a radical break with the past, the second, over time, resulted in the extent of the break being compromised.

At war's end, anti-Fascist unity was paramount and was expressed in the formation of a government of national solidarity that comprised all the national political parties, including the left (Communists, PCI; Socialists, PSIUP, later PSI; Actionists[2]). The concrete outcome and symbol of this unity was the 1948 Constitution, which was drafted between 1946 and 1948 by a freely elected Constituent Assembly, after the abolition of the monarchy by referendum. The anti-Fascist basis of the Constitution symbolizes Italy's revolutionary break with the past and the outcome of the Resistance and war of liberation against Fascism. The Constitution 'is indissolubly connected with antifascism, both theoretically and historically. It is antifascist by definition i.e. by its very nature as a democratic constitution, inasmuch as it is composed of the fundamental rights and democratic rules that were denied by Fascism and indeed represent the negation of Fascism. It is antifascist also because it originated, historically, from the Resistance. Anti-fascism is thus its genetic and constitutive element' (Ferrajoli 1996: 465). At the same time, the Constitution marked a break with the liberal order that preceded Fascism (Barbagallo 1994a: 110–11). Forged through an agreement between three mass parties (the Christian Democrats, DC; the PCI; and the PSIUP/PSI), the Constitution went beyond the old liberal conception of the *stato di diritto* ('state of law'), which had traditionally drawn a sharp distinction between the sphere of politics (government, parliament) and that of society and the economy, and which had identified the former with the state administration.

Yet, while there was a break with fascism and the birth of a modern parliamentary democracy at a general level (and while one can trace anti-fascism in specific parts of the Constitution), the actual drafting of the founding document was influenced as much, if not more, by a second fault line: that of anti-communism. This fault line preceded the development of the Cold War, but was gradually exacerbated and expanded by it, to the point of overshadowing anti-Fascist unity. The forces that emerged in the post-Fascist period were broadly divided into two camps. The first camp consisted of those groups (Communists, Socialists, Actionists, generally supported by the working class) that wished to enact a political and social revolution on the basis of the Resistance, or at least to enact a radical reform of the socio-economic order. The second camp consisted of those groups (the Christian Democrats and Liberals (PLI) supported by the Allies, the Monarchy, the Vatican, the large industrial groups and the existing state personnel) that wished to retain the *status quo*, or at least some version of it, by resisting any structural changes to the old order. The power struggle was played out on two levels: day-to-day government, on the one hand, and the drafting of the Constitution, on the other.

At the first level (day-to-day government), despite the aspirations of the Resistance movement to achieve a break with the past, the conservative forces gradually re-established control, and 'a political, administrative and economic settlement emerged, far more moderate than had seemed conceivable in April 1945' (Woolf 1972b: 222). This was facilitated by the willingness of the left to compromise on many issues or not to oppose developments taking place. Purges of state personnel were brought to an end, and the bureaucracy rapidly expanded. The Constituent Assembly was denied legislative powers and the right to decide on the Monarchy's fate. The Prefects of the Committees of National Liberation in the North were swept away. The capitalist economy was refounded through the return of industrialists who had fled during the Liberation and the emergence of powerful industrial groups reminiscent of the liberal and Fascist orders. Some Fascist corporative structures and state monopolies survived, and these, combined with informal agreements which restricted competition, provided the foundations for the development of large state and private monopolies, which exploited both American aid and the economic boom of the 1950s. Accusations of patronage and corruption quickly became rife (Woolf 1972b: 240–1).

The left's (reluctant) acceptance of this 'inverting' situation derived from two factors. On the one hand, the Communist leader Togliatti recognized the constraints imposed by the international situation, and especially the American pressure being brought to bear on the Prime Minister, De Gasperi. On the other hand, Togliatti's optimism about the progressive nature of Christian Democracy and the likely continuation of the grand coalition of three major parties was misguided (Ginsborg 1990: ch. 3). Certainly, by the time the elections to the Constituent Assembly were held in 1946, the forces of conservatism had largely reasserted themselves, and the so-called wind from the North was spent. De Gasperi's decision in May 1947 to exclude the two main left-wing parties from government completed this trend, constituting 'an important moment in the process by which Christian Democracy acquired a conservative label and Italian politics were polarized into two irreconcilable, almost uncommunicating, extremes' (Mack Smith 1997: 423).

This increased the importance of what could be achieved in the drafting of the Constitution (the second level). It is here that the differences between the two camps' conceptions of the post-war order surfaced most clearly. True, the common fear was, perhaps inevitably, the 'dictatorial abuse of executive power' (Allum 1993: 13), but there was disagreement on how best this could be prevented. The Christian Democrats and their allies wanted a Constitution characterized by a strong system of 'checks and balances'. They argued that the Fascist experience had demonstrated the dangers of concentrating too much power in one branch of government. However, it was evident that the position was also motivated by fear of a left-wing majority attempting to drive through socialist reforms. They also wanted recognition of Catholicism as

* * *

...es from the bank of
...e Titania lay asleep, a group
...had gathered in secret to
...ay that they meant to perform
...eseus after his wedding. One
..., a weaver called Bottom, was
...ehind a tree, waiting to appear
...when he heard his cue.

"I'll show them how it's done!" Bottom said to himself. "When the Duke sees what a fine actor I am, he'll give me a purse of gold, or my name's not Nick Bottom!"

"Because at last I have found my own true love," said Lysander. "Helena, can't you see how much I love you?"

Helena stepped back, laughing nervously. "Don't be silly, Lysander!" she said. "You love Hermia...don't you?"

"Hermia, who is she?" scoffed Lysander, scrambling to his feet. "How could I love anyone but you, with your eyes like stars, your hair as black as ravens' wings, and your skin as soft as...?"

"That's quite enough of that!" said Helena. "This is some sort of midsummer madness!"

"Madness? Yes, I'm mad!" said Lysander. "Mad with love for you! Come to my arms, and cool the fires of my passion with your kisses!"

He moved towards Helena, but she turned and fled. Lysander followed her, shouting, "There's no escape from love, Helena! This was meant to be!"

Their loud footsteps wo
are you?" sh
wander off o
might be eate
The very tho
and she sat u
come to that
"I'm coming
can be eaten

Not five pac
violets wher
of Athenian
rehearse a p
for Duke Th
of the actor

He glanced up,
and saw a strange
orange light
circling the tree.
"Now what's
that, I wonder?"
he muttered.
"A firefly
perhaps?"

It was Puck.
He had noticed
the actors as he
flew by on his
way back to
Oberon, and had seen
a chance to make mischief.
"Behold, the Queen's new love!" he said.
Magic sparks showered down from his
fingertips on to the weaver.

Immediately Bottom's face began to sprout hair, and his nose and ears grew longer and longer. His body was unchanged, so Bottom had no idea that anything was wrong, until he heard his cue and stepped out from behind a tree.

Bottom had meant his entrance to be dramatic, and it certainly was. The other actors took one look at the donkey-headed monster coming towards them, and raced away screaming and shouting.

"What's the matter with them?" said
Bottom, scratching his chin. "My word,
my beard has grown quickly today! I'll
need a good shave before the performance
tomorrow!" He paced this way and that,
puzzling out why his friends had left in
such a hurry. "O-o-h! I see-haw, hee-
haw!" he said at last. "They're trying to
frighten me by leaving me alone in the
wood in the dark! Well it won't work!
It takes more than that to frighten a man
like me-haw, hee-haw!"

And to prove how brave he was, Bottom began to sing. His voice was part human, part donkey and it sounded like the squealing of rusty hinges. It woke Queen Titania from her sleep on the bank of violets. "Do I hear an angel singing?" she said, and raised herself on one elbow and gazed at Bottom. "Adorable human, I have fallen wildly in love with you!" she told him.

"Really?" said Bottom, not the least alarmed by the sudden appearance of the Fairy Queen. He was sure it was all part of the trick his friends were playing.

"Sit beside me, so I can stroke your long, silky ears!" Titania purred. "My servants will bring you anything you desire."

"I wouldn't say no to some supper," said Bottom. "Nothing fancy – a bale of hay or a bag of oats would suit me fine!"

From up above came the sound of Puck's laughter, like the pealing of tiny bells.

* * *

Oberon's laughter set every owl in the
wood hooting. "My proud Queen, in love
with a donkey?" he cried. "Well done,
Puck! Titania will think twice before she
defies me again! But what of the humans?"

"I did as you commanded, master," said Puck. "I found them…"

A voice made him turn his head, and he saw Demetrius stamping along the path, dragging Hermia by the arm.

"That is the fellow!" said Oberon. "But who is that with him?"

"He is not the one I cast the spell on!" Puck yelped.

"Quickly," said Oberon. "Make yourself invisible before they see us!"

✳ ✳ ✳

Hermia was thoroughly miserable. Everything had gone wrong: she had found Demetrius instead of Lysander, and Demetrius was in such a foul temper that she feared the worst. "Oh, where is Lysander?" she wailed. "You've killed him, haven't you, you brute?"

With a weary groan, Demetrius let Hermia go and slumped to the ground. "I haven't touched your precious Lysander!" he yawned. "Now stop whining and get some sleep. When it's light, we'll find our way out of this accursed wood."

"I won't rest until I find Lysander!" Hermia said defiantly.

"Just as you wish," said Demetrius. "I'm too tired to argue any more."

He lay back among the ferns and closed his eyes. He heard Hermia walking away, and then he fell into a deep sleep.

Moonlight shifted and shivered as Oberon and Puck reappeared. "This is the man," said Oberon, peering down at Demetrius. "Search the wood for a black-haired maiden, and bring her here. When she is close by I will put magic juice in his eyes and wake him."

"Yes, master! But tell me, is human love always so complicated?" Puck asked curiously.

"Just do as I have commanded!" snapped Oberon.

✳ ✳ ✳

Helena was still running, with Lysander just a few steps behind her. So many bewildering things had happened to her, that when an orange light appeared above the path in front of her, she was not surprised – in fact, a curious idea suddenly popped into her mind – Puck's magic had put it there. Helena became convinced that if she followed the light, it would lead her

back to Athens, and sanity. Over streams and through clearings the light led her, until at last she came to a deep thicket of ferns, where she paused for breath.

"Helena, marry me!" she heard Lysander shout.

"I don't want you!" she shouted back. "I want Demetrius!"

"And here I
am, my love!"
said Demetrius,
springing up out
of the ferns nearby, his
eyes glowing with magic.
"Hold me, let me melt in your sweetness!"

Helena did not bother to wonder why
Demetrius had changed his mind: her
dreams had come true, and she was about

to rush into his arms
when Lysander ran
between them.
"Keep away
from her,
Demetrius!"
Lysander
said hotly.
"Helena is mine!"

"Lysander...is that you?" called a voice, and Hermia came stumbling out of the bushes. Brambles had torn the hem of her dress, and there were leaves and twigs stuck in her hair. "Thank the gods you're safe!" she said, weeping for joy. "Why did you leave me, my only love?"

"Because I can't bear the sight of you!" said Lysander. "I want to marry Helena."

"So do I!" Demetrius exclaimed. "And since she can't marry both of us, we'll have to settle the matter, man to man!"

He pushed Lysander's chest, knocking him backwards, then Lysander pushed Demetrius.

Hermia stared at Helena, her eyes blazing. "You witch! You've stolen my Lysander!" she screeched.

"I haven't stolen anybody!" Helena replied angrily. "This is all some cruel trick, isn't it? The three of you plotted together to make a fool of me – and I thought you were my friend!"

"Our friendship ended when you took Lysander away from me!" snarled Hermia.

And there might have been a serious fight, if Oberon had not cast a sleeping spell on all four of them. They dropped to the ground like ripe apples, Hermia falling close to Lysander and Helena collapsing at Demetrius's side.

Oberon and
Puck appeared
magically
beside them.
"Smear their eyes
with fairy juice!"
said Oberon. "This knot
of lovers will unravel when they wake."

As Puck hurried about his task, the air
was filled with the singing of fairy voices.
"The Queen!" Puck muttered in alarm.
"The Queen is coming!"

Titania did not notice Puck and Oberon, or
the sleeping lovers. She could see nothing
but Bottom, whose jaws were stretched
open in a wide yawn. "Are you weary,
dearest one?" she asked him tenderly. "Rest
with me on these soft ferns."

"I feel a powerful sleep coming over me-haw, hee-haw!" said Bottom.

"Fairies, leave us!" ordered Titania.

The fairies flew away, leaving bright trails in the air. Titania cradled Bottom's head in her lap, and they both dozed.

Oberon and Puck crept close. Puck began to grin, but he stopped when he saw the sorrow in his master's eyes.

"There is no laughter in this!" Oberon sighed. "How I long for Titania to smile at me, as she smiled at this creature, and to feel her soft arms around me as I sleep! Break the spell on the human, Puck, while I deal with the Queen."

Oberon moved his hands, weaving shadows into magic as he chanted:

"Be the way you used to be,
See the way you used to see,
Wake, my Queen, and come to me!"

Titania opened her eyes, and when she saw Oberon she flew into his arms. "I am so glad that you are here, my love!" she said. "I had the strangest dream! I dreamed that I had fallen in love with a..."

"We will never quarrel again," Oberon promised. "Keep your page – have fifty pages if you wish! What does it matter, as long as we are together?"

Puck saw that the sky was getting lighter. "It's almost dawn, master!" he warned.

"Then we must leave!" said Oberon, and he, Titania and Puck faded into the pale morning light.

When the sun rose, its light woke
Demetrius and Helena, who fell in love at
first sight, then Lysander and Hermia,
who fell in love all over again. There was
much smiling, sighing and kissing, and
soon Demetrius said, "Today is Duke
Theseus's wedding day, as well as mine
and Helena's. Come, my friends, the priest
can marry us all at the same ceremony!"

And the lovers hurried off towards
Athens, laughing every step of the way,
the paths of their true love running
smoothly at last.

And as for Bottom, he woke some time later and clambered stiffly to his feet. "I thought I was…!" He mumbled. "I thought I had…!" Anxiously, he felt his face and ears, and then sighed with relief.

"What a midsummer night's dream!" he exclaimed. "I'll write a poem about it, and read it to Duke Theseus and his bride, and the Duke will say: 'Well done, noble Bottom! Here's some gold for you!'"

And he stumbled away through the ferns, making up lines of poetry and reciting them out loud as he went.

The eye of man hath not heard, the ear of man hath not seen, man's hand is not able to taste, his tongue to conceive, nor his heart to report what my dream was.

Bottom; IV.i.

Love and Magic in
A Midsummer Night's Dream

In *A Midsummer Night's Dream* Shakespeare brings together two worlds: the human world of Athens, and the fairy world of the woods outside the city. One world is ruled by law, the other by magic, and in both worlds trouble is brewing.

In the woods outside Athens, Oberon and Titania are busy arguing over a page boy. Meanwhile Demetrius, who is as stubborn as Oberon, is insisting on marrying Hermia, even though she loves someone else. Add a group of bickering actors, and Puck, a mischievous sprite, and madness follows.

The humans are made to love the wrong partners, and Titania falls in love with one of the actors, who has the head of a donkey!

When the human lovers begin to fight one another, the play comes close to tragedy, but magic sets things right. The humans find their true loves and Oberon realises that his love for Titania is stronger than his pride.

The Elizabethans believed in a 'midsummer madness' that was caused by the heat of the summer sun, and many of the characters in *A Midsummer Night's Dream* behave as if they have been touched by this madness.

The fairy world and the human world are thrown into chaos by love, and Shakespeare pokes fun at how lovers behave. And in the character of Bottom he makes fun of actors – and even playwrights like himself too!

Shakespeare and the Globe Theatre

Some of Shakespeare's most famous plays were first performed at the Globe Theatre, which was built on the South Bank of the River Thames in 1599.

Going to the Globe was a different experience from going to the theatre today. The building was roughly circular in shape, but with flat sides: a little like a doughnut crossed with a fifty-pence piece. Because the Globe was an open-air theatre, plays were only put on during daylight hours in spring and summer. People paid a penny to stand in the central space and watch a play, and this part of the audience became known as 'the groundlings' because they stood on the ground. A place in the tiers of seating beneath the thatched roof, where there was a slightly better view and less chance of being rained on, cost extra.

The Elizabethans did not bath very often and the audiences at the Globe were smelly. Fine ladies and gentlemen in the more expensive seats sniffed perfume and bags of sweetly-scented herbs to cover the stink rising from the groundlings.

There were no actresses on the stage; all the female characters in Shakespeare's plays would have been acted by boys, wearing wigs and make-up. Audiences were not well-behaved. People clapped and cheered when their favourite actors came on stage; bad actors were jeered at and sometimes pelted with whatever came to hand.

Most Londoners worked hard to make a living and in their precious free time they liked to be entertained. Shakespeare understood the magic of the theatre so well that today, almost four hundred years after his death, his plays still cast a spell over the thousands of people that go to see them.

Orchard Classics
Shakespeare Stories

RETOLD BY ANDREW MATTHEWS
ILLUSTRATED BY TONY ROSS

As You Like It	978 1 84616 187 2	£4.99
Hamlet	978 1 84121 340 8	£4.99
A Midsummer Night's Dream	978 1 84121 332 3	£4.99
Antony and Cleopatra	978 1 84121 338 5	£4.99
The Tempest	978 1 84121 346 0	£4.99
Richard III	978 1 84616 185 8	£4.99
Macbeth	978 1 84121 344 6	£4.99
Twelfth Night	978 1 84121 334 7	£4.99
Henry V	978 1 84121 342 2	£4.99
Romeo & Juliet	978 1 84121 336 1	£4.99
Much Ado About Nothing	978 1 84616 183 4	£4.99
Othello	978 1 84616 184 1	£4.99
Julius Caesar	978 1 40830 506 5	£4.99
King Lear	978 1 40830 503 4	£4.99
The Merchant of Venice	978 1 40830 504 1	£4.99
The Taming of the Shrew	978 1 40830 505 8	£4.99

Orchard Books are available from all good bookshops.